The story made me feel grateful … there's help for Floss.

Y1 pupil, Werneth Primary School,
Oldham

This is an important topic to talk about … different year groups can read it … it's about physical and mental bullying; the scenarios can happen in real life.

The message is that you should never be controlled.

Y6 pupils, Crab Lane Primary School,
Manchester

This book does a great job of showing how domestic abuse and coercive control can manifest and the impact they can have on children and young people. It is a very useful resource for education and social care professionals working with families.

Kate Stanley, Director of Strategy,
Policy and Evidence at NSPCC

T0087654

FLOSS AND THE BOSS

Catherine Lawler works as a training consultant for a Safeguarding Children's Partnership. She has extensive experience supporting children, young people and families. She has worked as a children's therapist, specialising in domestic abuse. She has developed resources on bullying, peer-on-peer abuse and children accessing sexualised imagery.

Abigail Sterne is a senior educational psychologist working in schools in Manchester and is a former teacher. She works closely with Central Manchester Child and Adolescent Mental Health Services (CAMHS) and has worked with fostering and adoption services.

Catherine and Abigail are co-authors of *Domestic Violence and Children: A Handbook for Schools and Early Years Settings* (Routledge, 2010). They have developed domestic abuse and safeguarding training packages for education and social care services. They wrote and delivered initial training for key adults for Operation Encompass, whereby key trained adults in schools receive prompt police notifications about abusive incidents. For this they received Commander's Certificates from Devon and Cornwall Constabulary.

Nicky Armstrong, B.A. (Hons) Theatre Design, M.A. Slade School of Fine Art, has illustrated 30 books which have been translated and published in seven countries. She has achieved major commissions in both mural and fine art painting.

Floss and the Boss

Catherine Lawler and Abigail Sterne

Illustrated by Nicky Armstrong

Routledge
Taylor & Francis Group

LONDON AND NEW YORK

First published 2021
by Routledge
2 Park Square, Milton Park, Abingdon, Oxon OX14 4RN

and by Routledge
52 Vanderbilt Avenue, New York, NY 10017

Routledge is an imprint of the Taylor & Francis Group, an informa business

British Library Cataloguing-in-Publication Data
A catalogue record for this book is available from the British Library

Library of Congress Cataloging-in-Publication Data
Names: Lawler, Catherine, author. | Sterne, Abigail, author. | Armstrong, Nicky, illustrator.
Title: Floss and the boss : helping young children learn about domestic abuse and coercive control / Catherine Lawler and Abigail Sterne ; illustrated by Nicky Armstrong.
Description: Milton Park, Abingdon, Oxon ; New York, NY : Routledge, 2020.
Identifiers: LCCN 2020008414 (print) | LCCN 2020008415 (ebook) |
    ISBN 9780367510794 (paperback) | ISBN 9781003052357 (ebook)
Subjects: LCSH: Child abuse--Juvenile literature. | Dogs--Juvenile literature.
Classification: LCC HV6626 .L387 2020 (print) | LCC HV6626 (ebook) |
    DDC 362.76--dc23
LC record available at https://lccn.loc.gov/2020008414
LC ebook record available at https://lccn.loc.gov/2020008415

ISBN: 978-0-367-51079-4 (pbk)
ISBN: 978-1-003-05235-7 (ebk)

Typeset in Bembo
by Servis Filmsetting Ltd, Stockport, Cheshire

Floss was called Floss because she looked like

a big ball of candy floss.

Every day Floss and Mum walked through the park to Doggy Daycare and met up with their friends. Floss loved Doggy Daycare and bounced in with the other puppies.

Back at home, after Doggy Daycare, Floss found her best friend Houdini the hamster. Houdini loved to hide, especially in Floss's fur.

At night, Mum settled Floss with a bedtime story.

Floss's eyes started to close, she felt warm, fuzzy and safe

and fell fast asleep.

One day, Mum said 'Meet Boss, Floss.'

Boss showed Floss and Mum his tricks and made them laugh. Boss could roll over, play dead *and* spin on his head.

Boss said he wanted to look after Mum and Floss. They went

to the park; Boss met their friends, and they shared the food.

Soon, Boss came to live with Floss and Mum. Boss said he could keep them safe and show them how to have fun.

But as Autumn changed to Winter, Boss changed too.

There was nice Boss … and there was scary Boss who

started growling … Boss could just give *the look* and Floss

and Mum knew what that meant. Floss was confused and

felt uh-oh feelings.

19

Boss started bossing … and making new rules:

Boss eats first.

Play quietly … or stop! Houdini stays locked in his cage.

No park without Boss.

No time for bedtime stories with Mum.

21

When Mum forgot the rules, Boss gave her a nasty nip.

It frightened Floss to see such a terrible thing.

Sometimes Floss felt cold and prickly.

Sometimes her tummy and head hurt.

Sometimes eating gave her a yucky feeling.

Sometimes she couldn't sleep and woke at night
with the wobblies.

Floss didn't bounce into Doggy Daycare anymore.

She wanted to stay at home with Mum. That's the only

place she wanted to be.

She worried about the nasty nip.

She was grumpy and sometimes got angry with her friends.

But kind Wagtail noticed Floss had changed.

'What's giving you the wobblies, Floss?'

At first, Floss couldn't speak to Wagtail. She was worried about what would happen.

But Wagtail was calm and friendly. Wagtail liked Floss and Floss liked Wagtail. Soon, Floss told Wagtail about Boss; about the cold pricklies and the uh-oh feelings. 'Oh, no wonder you've got the grumpies, Floss. How scary for you. Thank you for being brave and telling me.'

Then Wagtail talked to Mum and to others who might help.

It helped Mum to know how Floss was feeling.

Mum loved Floss and she also found it hard to talk

about her own wobbly feelings.

Wagtail had some good ideas about how to help Floss.
Wagtail showed Floss some things to do with the
jumbled-up feelings and the uh-ohs.

Then Floss felt a little bit better. She knows that what grown-up dogs do can never be a puppy's fault. She has lots of animals who listen, understand and care about her.

What are your good ideas to help Floss?